Revised Edition

Vocal Selections

PASSION

Music and Lyrics by
Stephen Sondheim

Book by
James Lapine

Live dramatic performance rights for "Passion" are represented exclusively by
Music Theatre International (MTI)
421 West 54th Street, New York, NY 10019.
www.MTIshows.com
For further information, please call (212) 541-4684
or email: Licensing@MTIshows.com

ISBN 978-1-4234-7265-0

RILTING MUSIC, INC.

EXCLUSIVELY DISTRIBUTED BY

HAL•LEONARD®
CORPORATION
7777 W. BLUEMOUND RD. P.O. BOX 13819 MILWAUKEE, WI 53213

Visit Hal Leonard Online at
www.halleonard.com

STEPHEN SONDHEIM wrote the music and lyrics for *Road Show* (2008), *Passion* (1994), *Assassins* (1991), *Into the Woods* (1987), *Sunday in the Park with George* (1984), *Merrily We Roll Along* (1981), *Sweeney Todd* (1979), *Pacific Overtures* (1976), *The Frogs* (1974), *A Little Night Music* (1973), *Follies* (1971, revised in London, 1987), *Company* (1970), *Anyone Can Whistle* (1964), and *A Funny Thing Happened on the Way to the Forum* (1962), as well as lyrics for *West Side Story* (1957), *Gypsy* (1959), *Do I Hear A Waltz?* (1965), and additional lyrics for *Candide* (1973). *Side by Side by Sondheim* (1976), *Marry Me A Little* (1981), *You're Gonna Love Tomorrow* (1983), and *Putting It Together* (1992) are anthologies of this work as a composer and lyricist. For films, he composed the scores of *Stavisky* (1974) and *Reds* (1981) and songs for *Dick Tracy* (1990), for which he won an Academy Award. He also wrote songs for the television production "Evening Primrose" (1966), co-authored the film *The Last of Sheila* (1973) and the play *Getting Away With Murder* (1996), and provided incidental music for the plays *The Girls of Summer* (1956), *Invitation to a March* (1961), and *Twigs* (1971). He won Tony Awards for Best Score for a Musical for *Passion*, *Into the Woods*, *Sweeney Todd*, *A Little Night Music*, *Follies*, and *Company*. All of these shows won the New York Drama Critics Circle Award, as did *Pacific Overtures* and *Sunday in the Park with George*, the latter also receiving the Pulitzer Prize for Drama (1985). He received a special 2008 Tony Award for Lifetime Achievement in the Theatre. Mr. Sondheim was born in 1930 and raised in New York City. He graduated from Williams College, winning the Hutchinson Prize for Music Composition, after which he studied theory and composition with Milton Babbitt. He is on the Council of the Dramatists Guild, the national association of playwrights, composers, and lyricists, having served as its president from 1973 to 1981, and in 1983 was elected to the American Academy of Arts and Letters. In 1990 he was appointed the first Visiting Professor of Contemporary Theatre at Oxford University and in 1993 was a recipient of the Kennedy Center Honors.

Contents

PASSION

Music and Lyrics by Stephen Sondheim
Book by James Lapine

Stephen Sondheim and James Lapine's musical explores the nature of love, beauty, obsession, and social repression in 19th century Italy. Adapted from Ettore Scola's film, *Passione d'Amore* and I.U. Tarchetti's novel, *Fosca*, the show was written and composed as one long rhapsody, with no intermission, breaks for applause, or even specific song titles. Sondheim's most romantic and Romantic score reflects his love of Ravel and Rachmaninoff. Constantly shifting meter and subtly varied harmonics beautifully support quiet, conversational moments, contrasting with strident military drums and crashing waves of unrestrained emotion.

Major Productions

Broadway, Plymouth Theatre, 1994
Starring Donna Murphy, Jere Shea, Marin Mazzie
Directed by James Lapine
4 Tony Awards, including Best Musical, Best Score, and Best Book
6 Drama Desk Awards, including Outstanding Musical, Outstanding Music, Outstanding Lyrics, and Outstanding Book

London West End, Queen's Theatre, 1996
Starring Maria Friedman, Michael Ball, Helen Hobson
Directed by Jeremy Sams

Lincoln Center Concert, Rose Theatre, 2005
Starring Patti LuPone, Michael Cerveris, Audra McDonald
Directed by Lonny Price
Broadcast on PBS Live from Lincoln Center

Recordings

Original Broadway Cast Album, Angel Records, 1994
Grammy Award for Best Musical Show Album

London Concert Cast Album, First Night Records, 1997

Video

Broadway Cast 1995/PBS Great Performances 1996/Image Entertainment DVD 2003

Plot Synopsis
by Sean Patrick Flahaven

Milan, Italy, 1863. A handsome young man, Giorgio, is making love with his beautiful mistress, Clara. They collapse in each others' arms and reflect on how they met (**Happiness**). Giorgio, a soldier, reveals that he has been transferred to a remote military outpost. He vows to write, but Clara is upset. They begin to make love again.

The scene shifts to the dining room of the post's commanding officer, Colonel Ricci. He and his officers banter and complain about the food. Giorgio arrives and we learn that he is something of a war hero. In a reverie interrupting the action, Clara appears and reads Giorgio's **First Letter**. Hearing distant piano music pulls him back, and the Colonel explains that the player is his sickly cousin, Fosca. He offers to lend her books to read. The mail arrives with a letter from Clara (**Second Letter**), which is interrupted by Fosca screaming offstage. The Colonel makes excuses for her unsettling outbursts.

Later, during military exercises, Giorgio writes to Clara about the inanities of his new assignment (**Third Letter**). The other soldiers march off, and the camp physician, Doctor Tambourri, approaches Giorgio and tells him more about Fosca's condition, "a kind of medical phenomenon, a collection of many ills."

The officers attempt to interest Giorgio in a card game, but he demurs and reads a **Fourth Letter** from Clara. Their daydream is interrupted by the appearance of Fosca, who is young but ugly, thin, sallow, and nervous. She returns the books he lent her, but is awkward in conversation and takes offense at an innocent comment from Giorgio (**I Read**). She apologizes and offers to show him the gardens, but when they see a funeral procession out the window, Fosca screams and faints.

The next day, the Colonel, Doctor, Giorgio, and Fosca stroll in the garden. Giorgio attempts to cheer up Fosca, but is distracted by thoughts of Clara (**Love Like Ours**) and forgets to watch his words. Fosca reproaches him bitterly but then begs for friendship (**They Hear Drums**). Giorgio agrees and notices that her fever has risen. The Colonel leads her away.

Three days later, Giorgio and Clara exchange letters about his decision to avoid Fosca. Having written a letter to Giorgio complaining about his absence, Fosca makes a rare appearance in the dining hall and sits next to him. She tries to hold his hand under the table, much to his dismay. Giorgio asks the Colonel for five days' leave in Milan.

Early the next morning, Fosca accosts Giorgio as he is leaving. She throws herself at him, but he rebuffs her. To placate her, he promises to write to her the next day.

Fosca reads Giorgio's dismissive letter, intercut with Giorgio and Clara's reunion (**Trio**).

Giorgio returns and visits Fosca. They deal with each other dispassionately, and Fosca learns that Clara is married to another man. Giorgio immerses himself in military drills, but is called back to Fosca's room by the Doctor. She is allegedly dying, but after speaking to Giorgio, she rallies and asks him to write a letter to her, which she dictates (**I Wish I Could Forget You**). Before he leaves, she insists that he kiss her.

In the billiard room, the junior officers speculate that Giorgio is spending time with Fosca in order to win the Colonel's favor (**Soldiers' Gossip**). The Colonel thanks Giorgio for showing her favor, and tells him about how she arrived at her present state, having a victim of circumstance as an unattractive woman and having been ruined by the philandering, embezzling "Count Ludovic of Austria" (**Flashback**).

On a mountainside, in an attempt at solitude, Giorgio reads a letter from Clara in which she begins to express her doubts about their future together (**Sunrise Letter**). Fosca appears, having followed him. He angrily spurns her advances (**Is This What You Call Love?**). In response, she has another attack and Giorgio must carry her limp body in the rain back to the outpost.

On the parade ground, the soldiers march and comment on Giorgio's perceived affair with Fosca (**Soldiers' Gossip**). Meanwhile, Giorgio writhes in a fever dream of being smothered by Fosca (**Nightmare**). The Doctor awakens him and sends him off to Milan on sick leave. Clara is delighted at the prospect (**Forty Days**).

Before Giorgio can reach her, however, Fosca confronts him on the train and calmly explains her obsession (**Loving You**). He takes her back to the outpost and confronts the Doctor, who has encouraged her affection for Giorgio in a misguided attempt at treatment. The other soldiers drunkenly express their jealousy (**Soldiers' Gossip**) but Giorgio forgoes most of his sick leave.

In Milan with Clara, Giorgio tries to explain his growing sympathy for Fosca and also asks Clara to leave her husband for him. She refuses and says Giorgio is behaving erratically.

Giorgio arrives back at the outpost in time for the Christmas party. The Colonel is surprised to receive a letter reassigning Giorgio back to Milan. Fosca, in despair, throws herself at Giorgio in front of everyone, to their embarrassment. Giorgio also receives a **Farewell Letter** from Clara, ending their affair.

The Colonel, having discovered the love letter that Fosca dictated to Giorgio, assumes that he took advantage of her and challenges Giorgio to a duel, to take place in the morning. Giorgio, in distress, demands that the Doctor arrange for him to see Fosca.

In Fosca's room, Giorgio tells her about the end of his affair with Clara and proclaims his new love for Fosca (**No One Has Ever Loved Me**). Despite his concern for her physical condition, they make love.

In the morning, Giorgio and the Colonel duel with pistols. Giorgio, barely paying attention, accidentally shoots the Colonel, then has an emotional breakdown much like Fosca's earlier ones.

Later, Giorgio recuperates in a hospital and receives a package from the Doctor with a letter explaining that Fosca died three days after Giorgio last saw her, unaware of the duel from which the Colonel recovered. As Giorgio goes through the other papers, the past comes to life as in fragments of a dream. The package also contains a final letter from Fosca, in which she says that she is at peace, having been loved by Giorgio (**Finale**).

HAPPINESS

Music and Lyrics by
STEPHEN SONDHEIM

be se - duc - tive. ___ How quick-ly pit - y leads to

You pit - ied me. How quick-ly pit - y leads to

dim.

Tranquillo

poco rall. *a tempo*

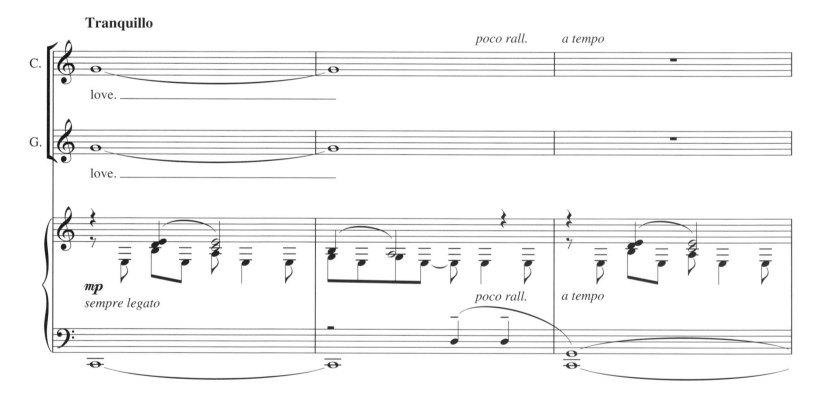

love. ___

love. ___

mp
sempre legato

poco rall. *a tempo*

CLARA: *poco rall.* *a tempo*

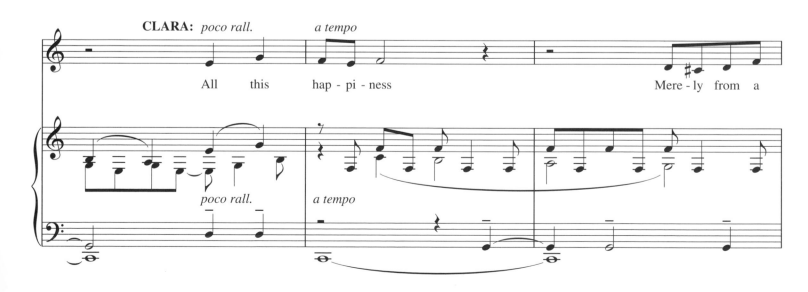

All this hap - pi - ness Mere - ly from a

poco rall. *a tempo*

Poco meno mosso

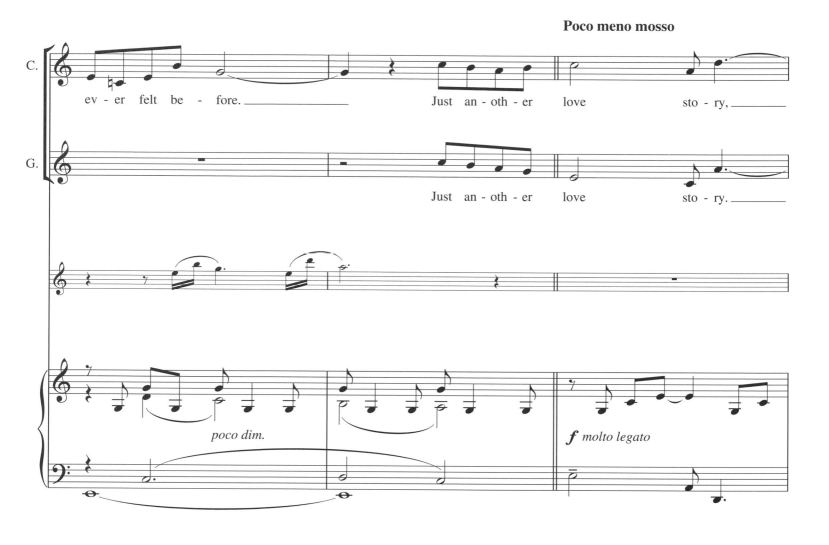

ev - er felt be - fore. _____ Just an - oth - er love sto - ry, _____

Just an - oth - er love sto - ry. _____

poco dim.

f *molto legato*

_____ That's what they would claim, An - oth - er sim - ple

_____ That's what they would claim, An - oth - er sim - ple

love sto - ry— _____ Are - n't all of them the same?

love sto - ry— _____ Are - n't all of them the same?

Poco rubato

No, but this is more, we feel more, This is so much

This is so much

more—! _____ Like ev - 'ry oth - er love sto - ry. _____

more—! _____ Like ev - 'ry oth - er love sto - ry. _____

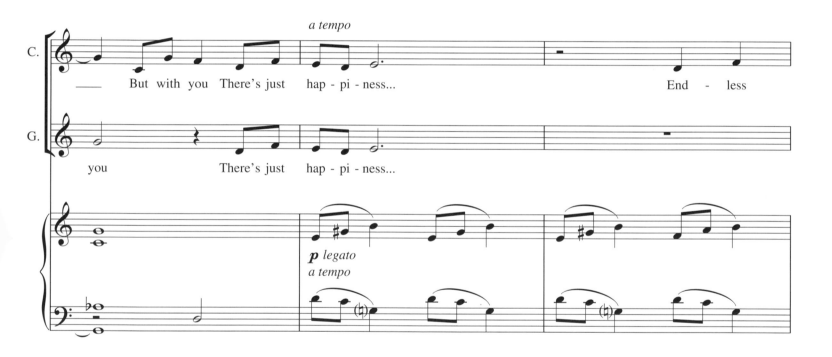

I READ

Music and Lyrics by
STEPHEN SONDHEIM

Larghetto (♩ = 76)

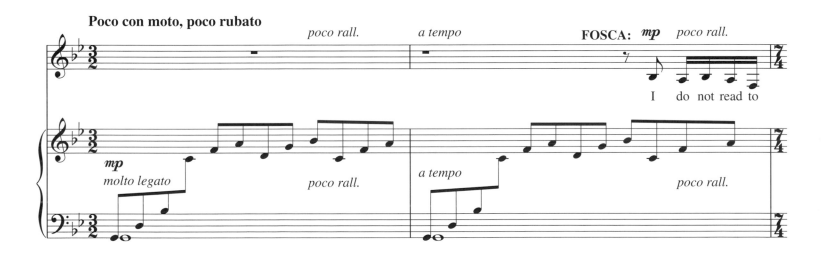

ech - oes. _____ I read to live, _____ To get a-way from

life. No, Cap-tain, I have no il - lu - sions. _____ I rec-og - nize the

Poco con moto

lim - its of my dreams. _____ I know how pain - ful dreams can be Un -

less you know _____ they're mere - ly dreams. There is a

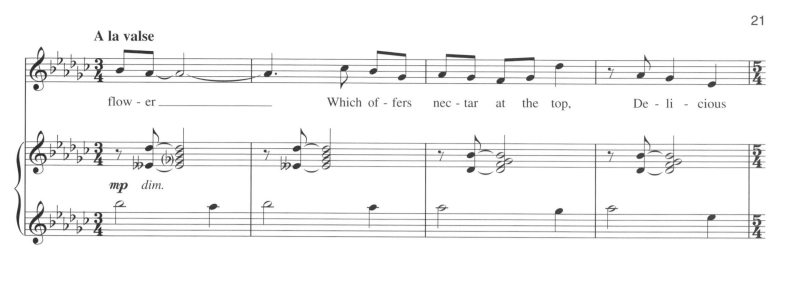

flow - er _____ Which of - fers nec - tar at the top, De - li - cious

nec - tar on the top, And bit - ter poi - son un - der - neath. The but - ter - fly that

stays too long _____ And drinks too deep is doomed _____ to die.

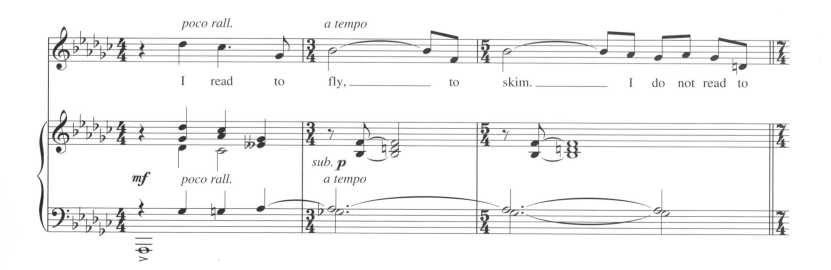

I read to fly, _____ to skim. _____ I do not read to

Con moto

cling to things, the more you love them, ___ The more the pain you suf - fer when they're

tak - en from you. ___ Ah, but if you have no ex - pec - ta - tions,

Cap - tain, You can nev - er have a dis - ap - point-ment.

TO FEEL A WOMAN'S TOUCH

Music and Lyrics by
STEPHEN SONDHEIM

touch...

Per-haps it was the dress, The fra-grance of her dress, The light per-fume of

silk That's warm from be-ing in the sun, That min-gles with a wom-an's own per-fume, The fra-grance of a

poco cresc.

LOVE LIKE OURS

Music and Lyrics by
STEPHEN SONDHEIM

C. thinks Ev-'ry-thing is pure, Ev-'ry-thing is beau-ti-ful,

G. thinks Ev-'ry-thing is pure, Ev-'ry-thing is beau-ti-ful,

C. Ev-'ry-thing is pos-si-ble, Love that fus-es

G. Ev-'ry-thing is pos-si-ble, Love that fus-es

cresc.

mf

C. Love that shuts a - way the world, That en - vel - ops my

G. Love that shuts a - way the world,

C. soul, That en - no - bles my life, Love that

G. That en - vel - ops your soul, Your life, Love that

dim.

THEY HEAR DRUMS

Music and Lyrics by
STEPHEN SONDHEIM

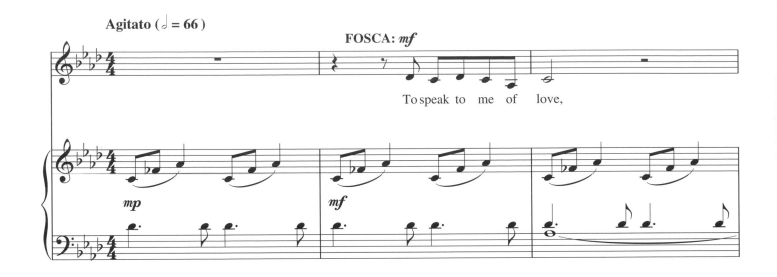

books, Your taste, Your sen - si - tiv - i - ty, I thought you'd un - der -

stand. The oth - ers... well, they're all a - like. Stu - pi - di - ty is

their ex - cuse, As ug - li - ness is mine. _____ But what is yours?

I've watched you from my win - dow. I saw you on the

day that you ar - rived._____ Per - haps it was the way you walked,___ The way you

spoke to your men, I knew that you were diff - 'rent then._____ I saw that you were

poco rall. *a tempo (agitato)*

kind and good.___ I thought you un - der - stood._____

espressivo

____ They hear drums, you hear mu - sic, As do

I WISH I COULD FORGET YOU

Music and Lyrics by
STEPHEN SONDHEIM

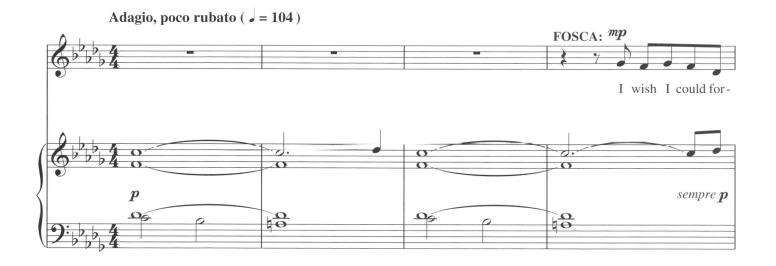

sight, But now I see you in a diff-'rent light. And though I can - not

poco rit.

poco cresc.

poco rit.

dim.

A tempo, non rubato

love you,_____ I wish that I could

p

cresc.

love you._____ For now I'm see - ing

love Like none I've ev - er known. A love as pure as

mf

mf legato

there you will stay. How could I ev - er wish you a - way? I see now I was

blind. And should you die to - mor - row,_____ An - oth - er thing I

see: Your love will live in me.

PASSION

SUNRISE LETTER

Music and Lyrics by
STEPHEN SONDHEIM

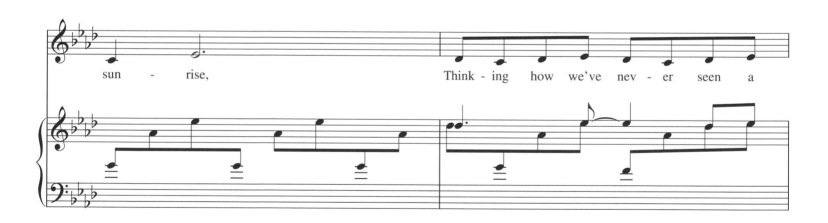

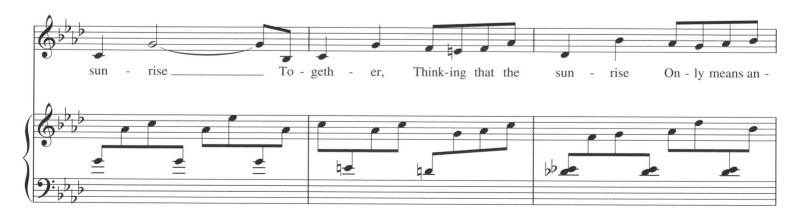

oth - er day ____ with - out   you, _____ And think - ing: Can our love sur -

vive   so much sep - a - ra - tion, Keep it - self a - live,   Much less

Poco meno mosso

thrive?   If on - ly   you were   here,   If I could feel your touch,   I would-n't have such

Poco con moto

fear. _____   If on - ly we had   more   than let - ters

swear, as I stare, There it is plain as day, A gray hair _____ Of which I was un-a-ware, Which is more than I can bear, Which I'm rip-ping out right now And am send-ing on to you As a mile-stone of my age, _____ As a turn-ing of the page. _____

leggiero

Per - haps when next we meet, I'll be a sor - ry

sight. You won't know who I am. My hair com - plete - ly

white, My face a mass of wrink - les, What will you feel then, My Gior - gio?

Time is now our en - e - my...

8vb

IS THIS WHAT YOU CALL LOVE?

Music and Lyrics by
STEPHEN SONDHEIM

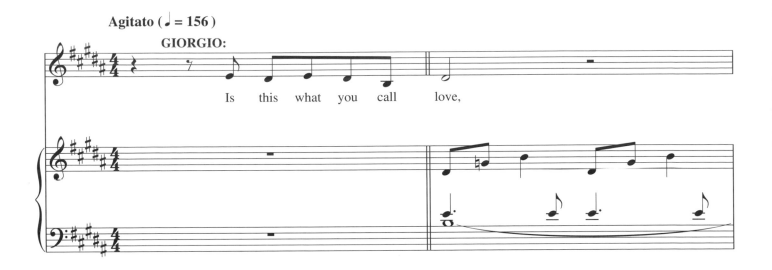

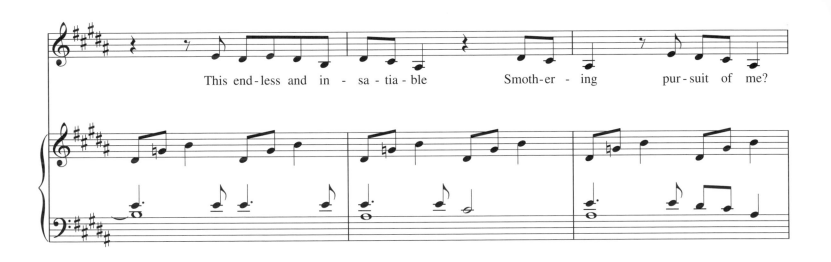

lone - ly, I'm sor - ry that you want me as you do. I'm sor - ry that I

fail to feel the way you wish me to feel. I'm sor - ry that you're

ill, I'm sor - ry you're in pain. I'm sor - ry that you

are - n't beau - ti - ful, But yes, I wish you'd go _____ a -

cern for what I feel, what I want? Love is what you

earn, _____ And re - turn, _____ When you

care for an - oth - er So much that the oth - er's set

free. _____ Don't you see, _____ Can't you un - der-

LOVING YOU

Music and Lyrics by
STEPHEN SONDHEIM

NO ONE HAS EVER LOVED ME
(Show Version)

Music and Lyrics by
STEPHEN SONDHEIM

Larghetto, rubato (♩ = 100)

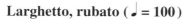

GIORGIO:

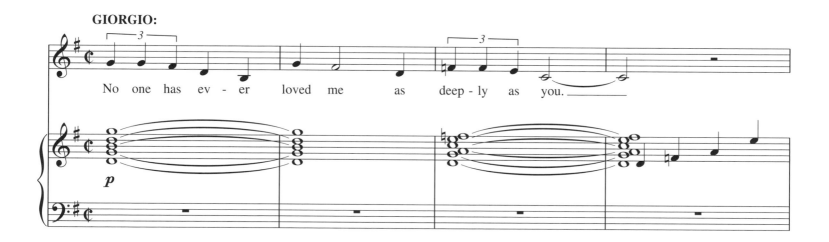

No one has ev - er loved me as deep - ly as you. _____

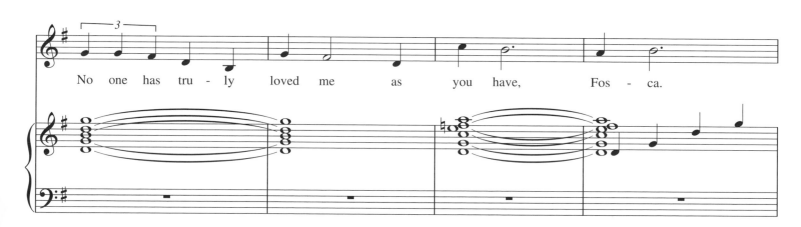

No one has tru - ly loved me as you have, Fos - ca.

NO ONE HAS EVER LOVED ME
(Original Version)

Music and Lyrics by
STEPHEN SONDHEIM

Con Passione (d'Amore), sempre rubato

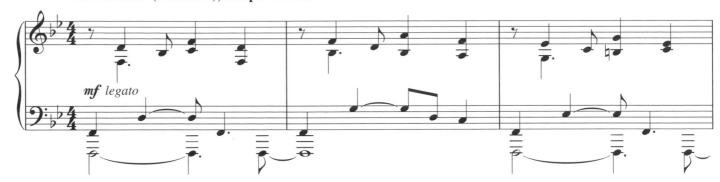

GIORGIO: *mf espressivo*

No one has ev - er loved me as

deep - ly as you. _____ No one has tru - ly

This song appears in a different version in the show (see "Show Version"). This is the composer's original version.

loved me as you have, Fos - ca.

Love with - out rea - son, Love with - out mer - cy, Love with - out pride or

shame. Love un - con - cerned with be - ing re - turned. No

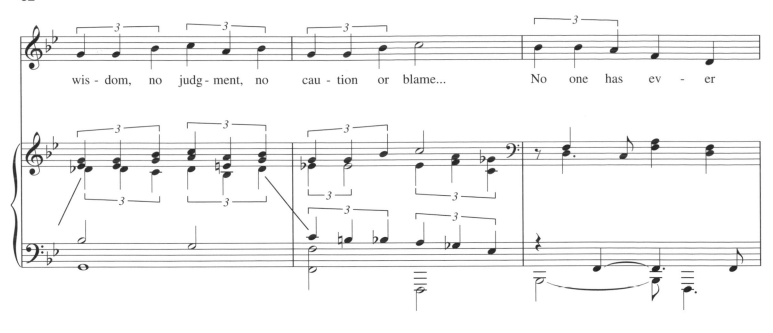

wis- dom, no judg - ment, no cau - tion or blame... No one has ev - er

known me as clear - ly as you.

No one has ev - er shown me that love al - lows ev - 'ry - thing,

Not pret - ty or safe or eas - y, But

more than I ev - er knew. Love with - in rea - son,

That is - n't love._____ And I've learned that from you.